It's My State!

ALASKA

The Last Frontier

Ruth Bjorklund, William McGeveran, and Laura L. Sullivan

Cavendish Square

New York

Published in 2016 by Cavendish Square Publishing, LLC
243 5th Avenue, Suite 136, New York, NY 10016

Website: cavendishsq.com

This publication represents the opinions and views of the author based on his or her personal experience, knowledge, and research. The information in this book serves as a general guide only. The author and publisher have used their best efforts in preparing this book and disclaim liability rising directly or indirectly from the use and application of this book.

CPSIA Compliance Information: Batch #CW16CSQ

All websites were available and accurate when this book was sent to press.

Library of Congress Cataloging-in-Publication Data

Bjorklund, Ruth.
Alaska / by Ruth Bjorklund, William McGeveran, and Laura L. Sullivan.
pages cm. — (It's my state!)
Includes bibliographical references and index.
ISBN 978-1-6271-3154-4 (hardcover) — ISBN 978-1-6271-3156-8 (ebook)
1. Alaska—Juvenile literature. I. McGeveran, William. II. Sullivan, Laura L. III. Title.

F904.3.B56 2016
979.8—dc23

2015017913

Editorial Director: David McNamara
Editor: Fletcher Doyle
Copy Editor: Rebecca Rohan
Art Director: Jeffrey Talbot
Designer: Joseph Macri
Senior Production Manager: Jennifer Ryder-Talbot
Production Editor: Renni Johnson
Photo Research: J8 Media

Printed in the United States of America

ALASKA ★ ★ ★ ★ ★
CONTENTS

★ State Flower: Forget-Me-Not

A native wildflower, the alpine forget-me-not became the state flower when Alaska gained statehood. Forget-me-nots bloom in rugged, sunny places at high elevation throughout Alaska in June and July. Each flower has five blue petals with a yellow center.

★ State Bird: Willow Ptarmigan

The willow ptarmigan is a relative of the Arctic grouse and lives in Alaska's **tundra** and high alpine areas. In the winter, its feathers turn white to help it hide from predators in the snow. In the summer and fall, its feathers turn brown to help it blend in with the ground and plants.

★ State Tree: Sitka Spruce

Found in the rain forests of southeastern Alaska, Sitka spruce can grow to heights of 200 feet (60 meters) or more. They may live for eight hundred years. Native Americans have used the tree to make totems, masks, charms, and other carvings. Today, the wood is also used for houses, ships, and musical instruments.

ALASKA

State Land Mammal: Moose

The moose is the largest member of the deer family. It can stand 7.5 feet (2.3 m) tall. Its partly flat antlers can grow to be 6 feet (1.8 m) wide. One moose can eat more than 40 pounds (18 kilograms) of twigs, bark, needles, tree roots, water plants, and willow and birch leaves each day.

State Marine Mammal: Bowhead Whale

Bowhead whales swim under the winter ice. They use their heads to smash through the ice to breathe. These whales can grow to be 60 feet (18 m) long and can weigh 120,000 pounds (54,500 kg). The US government has listed them as endangered. That means they are in danger of becoming extinct, or completely dying out.

State Dog: Alaskan Malamute

In 2010, after a campaign by students at the Polaris K–12 School in Anchorage, the Alaskan malamute was named the state dog. These animals, which Alaska's early peoples used thousands of years ago for hunting and hauling loads, have played a big role in Alaska history. They often serve as family pets, but they require a great deal of exercise.

The massive and beautiful Denali can be seen
from hundreds of miles away.

The Last Frontier

The great naturalist John Muir first saw Alaska's Glacier Bay in 1879. He described it as a "picture of icy wildness." The same words could be used today to describe Alaska itself, with its unspoiled natural wonders. The name Alaska comes from the Native Aleut people's word Alyeshka, meaning "the great land." Without a doubt, Alaska is great in its vast extent, rugged beauty, and energetic people.

A Vast State

Alaska is the biggest of the fifty states. It covers a land area of more than 570,000 square miles (1.5 million square kilometers), with more than 33,000 miles (53,000 kilometers) of shoreline. It is more than twice as large as Texas, which ranks second in size.

Its borders contain an amazing array of mountains, rivers, **glaciers**, volcanoes, islands, tundra, and rain forests. Alaska has more than three million lakes and several major rivers, including the Copper River and the Yukon. Huge coastal mountain ranges in the east and southeast rise up from sea level. To the north, the remote Brooks Range is the northernmost tip of the Rocky Mountains. Permanently frozen earth, ice floes and icebergs, eerie northern lights, days when the sun shines well past midnight, and more, are all part of Alaska's fantastic glory.

The Inside Passage, along the coast of southeastern Alaska, provides access to the state's scenery.

Most of Alaska is a peninsula in the northwest corner of North America. Two oceans, the Arctic and the Pacific, and three seas, the Bering, the Chukchi, and the Beaufort, surround the state on three sides. From the southwest corner of the Alaska Peninsula, a long chain of islands, the Aleutian Islands, extends to the southwest for 1,200 miles (1,900 km). From the southeast corner of the peninsula, a strip of land stretches south along the Pacific coast. This strip is called the Alaska Panhandle. The state is often divided into five regions. They range from southeastern Alaska (the Panhandle) to the Arctic North.

Alaska Borders

North:	Arctic Ocean
	Beaufort Sea
South:	Gulf of Alaska
	Pacific Ocean
	Canada
East:	Canada
West:	Bering Sea
	Chukchi Sea
	Pacific Ocean

Southeastern Alaska

Southeastern Alaska is a narrow, mountainous region along the coast of the Pacific Ocean. Thick rain forests of Sitka spruce, hemlock, ponderosa pine, and western cedar cover the mountains. A group of 1,100 offshore islands creates a system of canals, **fjords,** and channels called the Inside Passage. Cruise ships, ferries, tankers, tugs, barges, container ships, and pleasure boats travel through these scenic and protected waterways.

Southeastern Alaska is generally warmer and wetter than the rest of the state. Most years, 150 to 200 inches (380 to 500 centimeters) of rain or snow fall in the area. On the upper slopes of the mountains, snow falls year round. Rivers freeze and form glaciers that flow to the sea.

Alaska probably has about one hundred thousand glaciers in all, many of them in the southeast. They vary greatly in size. Only about six hundred have names. The largest glacier in the southeast, the Malaspina Glacier, covers about 1,500 square miles (3,900 sq km).

If you were to travel north through the Inside Passage, you would begin in the rain forests near the Misty Fjords National Monument. There, fog floats over narrow seas and steep cliffs. You would end your journey surrounded by icebergs and glaciers in Glacier Bay National Park. In geologic time, Glacier Bay is very new. Just over two hundred years ago, when British captain George Vancouver first sailed the area, he saw only "compact solid mountains of ice." Today, the glacier has melted to form a bay about 65 miles (105 km) long.

Most of the Panhandle, outside of Glacier Bay National Park, comprises Tongass National Forest. Covering 16.8 million acres (6.8 million hectares), this temperate **rain forest** is bigger than the whole state of West Virginia. It is the country's largest national forest by far.

The sun stays visible most of the day in summer in Sitka, on the Alaska Panhandle.

ALASKA
BOROUGH MAP

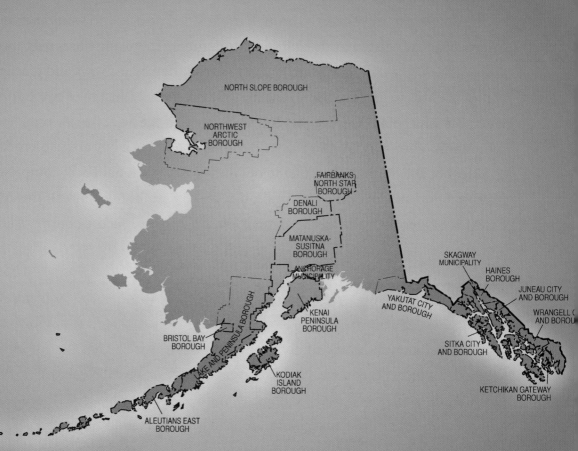

NORTH SLOPE BOROUGH

NORTHWEST ARCTIC BOROUGH

FAIRBANKS NORTH STAR BOROUGH

DENALI BOROUGH

MATANUSKA-SUSITNA BOROUGH

ANCHORAGE MUNICIPALITY

KENAI PENINSULA BOROUGH

SKAGWAY MUNICIPALITY

HAINES BOROUGH

JUNEAU CITY AND BOROUGH

WRANGELL C AND BOROU

YAKUTAT CITY AND BOROUGH

BRISTOL BAY BOROUGH

LAKE AND PENINSULA BOROUGH

SITKA CITY AND BOROUGH

KODIAK ISLAND BOROUGH

KETCHIKAN GATEWAY BOROUGH

ALEUTIANS EAST BOROUGH

ALASKA
POPULATION BY BOROUGH

Aleutians East Borough	3,141
Municipality of Anchorage	291,826
Bristol Bay Borough	997
Denali Borough	1,826
Fairbanks North Star Borough	97,581
Haines Borough	2,508
City and Borough of Juneau	31,275
Kenai Peninsula Borough	55,400
Ketchikan Gateway Borough	13,477
Kodiak Island Borough	13,592
Lake and Peninsula Borough	1,631
Matanuska-Susitna Borough	88,995
North Slope Borough	9,430
Northwest Arctic Borough	7,523
Petersburg Borough	3,273
City and Borough of Sitka	8,881
Municipality of Skagway	968
Unorganized Borough	78,149
City and Borough of Wrangell	2,369
City and Borough of Yakutat	662

Source: US Bureau of the Census, 2010

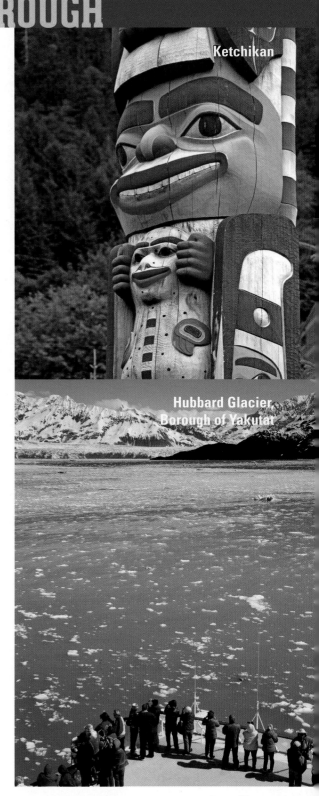

Ketchikan

Hubbard Glacier
Borough of Yakutat

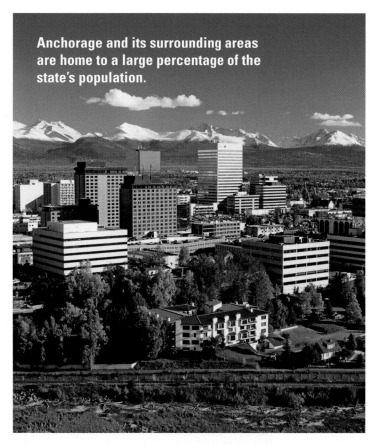
Anchorage and its surrounding areas are home to a large percentage of the state's population.

South-Central Alaska

More than half of the state's people live in south-central Alaska, which includes much of the Alaska Peninsula's southern coast and land north of the coast. This area contains snow-covered mountain ranges, seas bursting with marine life, busy fishing communities, farmlands, national parks, and the municipality of Anchorage, the state's city with the largest population. Huge amounts of precipitation fall, forming numerous glaciers. One glacier, the Bering, is bigger than the entire state of Rhode Island.

Wrangell-St. Elias National Park, located in south-central Alaska, is the biggest of Alaska's eight national parks and the largest in the United States. Inside the park, the St. Elias Mountains link with the Wrangell, Alaska, and Chugach mountain ranges. Brown bears, mountain goats, Dall sheep, bison, and other wild creatures roam the parkland, which covers 13.2 million acres (5.3 million ha).

Kenai Fjords, on the Kenai Peninsula, is the smallest of Alaska's national parks. There, more than 400 inches (1,000 cm) of snow fall each year on mountains, glaciers, and a sheet of ice called the Harding Icefield, which covers 300 square miles (775 sq km). The peninsula and the Gulf of Alaska are home to whales, seals, otters, and sea lions. Hardy mammals such as mountain goats, moose, bears, wolverines, and marmots live near the edges of the ice field.

The Aurora Borealis

Spring and autumn are the best times of year to look for the northern lights, or aurora borealis. When electrically charged particles from the sun enter the atmosphere above the polar regions, the gases in the atmosphere react by flashing colored beams of light across the northern sky.

Mount Griggs rises over the Valley of Ten Thousand Smokes.

Western Alaska

Western Alaska includes the Aleutian Islands and Kodiak Island off Alaska's southwest coast, and the region extends northward along the west side of the Alaska Peninsula. It is usually considered to stretch as far north as the Seward Peninsula on the west coast, just below the Arctic Circle.

Western Alaska is rich in wildlife. The wildlife refuge on Kodiak Island and nearby small islands is the only place in the world where you will find the Kodiak brown bear, the largest bear in the world. As many as thirty million seabirds migrate through this area. They include Emperor geese, murres, kittiwakes, cormorants, auklets, and puffins.

The Aleutians are a string of treeless, windswept islands. They stretch across the icy Bering Sea and North Pacific Ocean toward Russia. After leaving the busy Aleutian fishing port of Dutch Harbor, mariners sail over waters brimming with killer whales, gray whales, Steller sea lions, porpoises, and all five species of Pacific salmon. Many of the mountains are active volcanoes, such as those in the region called "Valley of Ten Thousand Smokes."

The 19-million-acre (8-million ha) Yukon Delta National Wildlife Refuge, on Alaska's west coast, is the biggest wildlife refuge in the world. There, the Yukon and the Kuskokwim Rivers spill into the sea, forming enormous **deltas**, or networks of streams, inlets, and deposits of rock and sediment. The area around these two river deltas also has more than forty thousand lakes. It is a wonderland for waterfowl.

★10★KEY SITES★ ★ ★

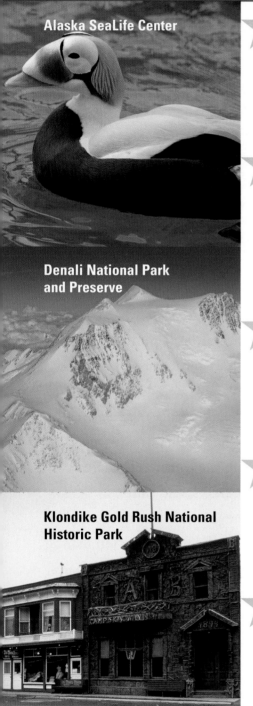

Alaska SeaLife Center

Denali National Park and Preserve

Klondike Gold Rush National Historic Park

1. Alaska Native Heritage Center

At this cultural and educational center in Anchorage, visitors can learn about the customs and traditions of Native Alaskans and visit replicas of traditional dwellings. Guides demonstrate songs, dances, and crafts.

2. The Alaska SeaLife Center

This "window to the sea" in Seward is Alaska's only public aquarium. It houses seals, sea lions, puffins, and other marine creatures, with a focus on Alaskan sea life. It also has active rescue and conservation programs and a cold-water research facility.

3. The Arctic Circle

Land and air tours visit this imaginary line, which sits at latitude 66 degrees, 33 minutes north. Above this line, the sun can stay visible for twenty-four hours a day near the summer solstice and doesn't rise at all near the winter solstice.

4. Denali National Park and Preserve

Within this park, which covers more than 6 million acres (2,428,113 ha), are wolves, brown bears, **caribou**, elk, and other wildlife, as well as Denali, the highest mountain in North America.

5. Klondike Gold Rush National Historic Park

In 1897–1898, thousands of men and women poured into the Klondike seeking gold. Visitors can learn about the **gold rush** in the historic district, hike the 33-mile (53.1 km) Chilkoot Trail, or take a train ride through the mountains.

6. Kodiak National Wildlife Refuge

This nearly 2-million-acre (809,371 ha) refuge encompasses islands in the Kodiak Archipelago in southwestern Alaska. The climate is wet and mild, and the environment is home to salmon, brown bears, foxes, and ermines.

7. Mendenhall Glacier

Stop by the Mendenhall Glacier Visitors Center for a wealth of information about the area and a chance to see a glacier calving, or having chunks break off into icebergs. Hiking and nature watching are also popular.

8. Mount Roberts Tramway

This tram, which runs from May through September, is located in Juneau. The cars make a steep climb, 1,800 feet (548 m) from the docks through the rain forest, to a park that offers hiking, great views, and cultural education.

9. Totem Heritage Center

Started as a way to save old **totem poles** and preserve the art of totem pole making, this center in Ketchikan allows guests to see totem poles of the Tlingit, Haida, and other tribes. Master carvers share their skill and knowledge.

10. University of Alaska Museum of the North

The museum building, located in Fairbanks, is designed to look like the Alaskan landscape. Inside are thousands of artifacts from indigenous cultures, as well as art, paleontology exhibits, and information on Alaskan life through the ages.

Kodiak National Wildlife Refuge

Mendenhall Glacier

Mount Roberts Tramway

North of these deltas, the Seward Peninsula juts across the Bering Strait. It ends only 56 miles (90 km) from Siberia in eastern Russia. The historic village of Nome rests on the southern coast of the peninsula, overlooking Norton Sound. On the north side, soaring sea cliffs, lagoons, lava beds, and hot springs are home to waterfowl and birds of prey such as bald eagles, hawks, falcons, and owls.

The Interior

The central region of Alaska, known as the Interior, is immense. The Interior begins at the Canadian border in the east and sweeps west to the Yukon Delta. It is bordered to the south by the Alaska Range and to the north by the Brooks Range.

The central part of the Interior is mostly tundra. The land is flat, treeless, and cold. Great rivers flow through the Interior, among them the Yukon, Kuskokwim, Tanana, Porcupine, Koyukuk, and Innoko. The Tanana flows past Fairbanks, the region's major city. In the Interior wilderness, salmon swim up rivers to breed, and giant trumpeter swans and rare sandhill cranes spend summers raising their young. Caribou, moose, bears, lynx, and wolves make their homes on the tundra, on mountain slopes, or in forests of birch, spruce, and aspen.

The Alaska Range serves as a barrier to the high winds that blow off the Gulf of Alaska.

Denali, which reverted to its Native name from Mount McKinley in 2015, is the tallest point in North America. At 20,320 feet (6,194 m), it towers over the other peaks in the Alaska Range and can be seen 200 miles (320 km) away. Climbers first reached the summit in 1913. Nowadays, several hundred people make it to the top each year.

The Arctic North

Northern Alaska looks cold and bleak, but it is really full of life. Lying north of the Arctic Circle, the Brooks Range runs east to west across the southern border of Alaska's Arctic North region. This range of high, jagged peaks is the northern tip of the continental divide and contains two national parks, Kobuk Valley and Gates of the Arctic. Rivers that flow from the Brooks Range are some of the wildest and most unspoiled in the world.

Spruce, fir, and pine trees grow on the south slope of the range. But because an average of no more than 10 inches (25 cm) of precipitation falls each year on the north side of the range, the region to the north known as the North Slope is nearly barren of trees. Scrubby shrubs, mosses, wildflowers, and lichens grow on the tundra. Underneath the surface soil of the tundra is a layer of **permafrost**, or permanently frozen earth. It cannot hold water, so plants with deep root systems cannot survive.

When the short Arctic spring comes, the snow and ice melt, and pools of water form above the permafrost layer. Wildflowers and grasses burst forth. Musk oxen, brown bears, foxes, wolves, and caribou, as well as birds from all over the world, move about the tundra. Along the coastline, rare marine mammals live among ice floes and along the coastal plain. They include Pacific walruses, polar bears, and bearded, ringed, and spotted seals, as well as beluga and gray whales, killer whales, and harbor porpoises.

Climate and Seasons

The coldest temperature ever recorded in the United States, –80 degrees Fahrenheit (–62 degrees Celsius), was measured at Prospect Creek Camp in Alaska's Brooks Range, on January 23, 1971. The average January temperature in Fairbanks is –10°F (–23°C). But in the southeast and south-central regions, the Pacific Ocean has a warming effect, and the Alaska Range blocks many cold, northerly winds. Temperatures range from around 20°F (–7°C) in winter to around 60°F (16°C) in summer.

Like the Aleutian Islands, the southern coastal areas are very wet. But the Aleutian Islands are colder, and the skies are gray and cloudy on an average of 355 days a year.

Surrounded by mountain ranges, Alaska's Interior has the most dramatic weather contrasts. During the summer, long days and sunny skies can raise temperatures above

90°F (32°C). In the winter, when days average only four hours of light, the temperature can drop to around −60°F (−50°C). The weather is fairly dry. Only about 12 inches (30 cm) of precipitation falls each year.

The Arctic region is even drier. Scientists call the area a frozen desert. The Arctic Ocean ices over in winter, as do the rivers flowing across the tundra, and a massive sheet of ice blankets the region. Winter temperatures average around −20°F (−30°C). Added wind chills can make it feel like −60°F (−50°C) or lower. Even during the summer months, temperatures in the Arctic North rarely get above 50°F (10°C).

At the Arctic Circle, the sun does not set during the summer solstice or rise during the winter solstice. Above the Arctic Circle, these periods of constant light and constant dark occur for a longer period of time.

In the northern Alaskan city of Barrow, for example, the summer sun stays in the sky, day and night, for eighty-four days. Even below the Arctic Circle, summer days are very long. In Anchorage, the sun sets well after 10 p.m. during most of the summer. Alaskans

The Short-Tailed Albatross

The endangered short-tailed albatross lives in Japan but flies as far as Alaska to feed in the rich Arctic waters. A century ago, there were millions of these giant seabirds. They almost became extinct due to the feather trade and entanglement in fishing lines. Thanks to conservation efforts, more than two thousand breeding pairs remain.

Wildflowers decorate the Arctic National Wildlife Refuge during the short summer.

love their long, light-filled summer days. But winter days are short, when there is any daylight at all. Barrow is without daylight for sixty-seven days each winter. People say that if you make it through a long, dark, cold Alaskan winter, you deserve the long beautiful days of an Alaskan summer.

Spring, like autumn, is very short, but dramatic. Along the Arctic coastline, the sea ice melts and splits into pieces called pack ice. These big ice floes provide the main hunting ground for polar bears. Elsewhere in Alaska, melting snow builds up huge amounts of slush and mud. Frozen rivers crack and thaw, sending water and chunks of ice downstream. Alaskans call the season "break up."

In the Wild

Alaska has more wild caribou than people. The state is also home to wolves, musk oxen, Dall sheep, sea otters, river otters, loons, snowy owls, and trumpeter swans. Some animals that are endangered or threatened (at risk of becoming endangered) in the lower forty-eight states thrive in Alaska. They include the bald eagle, gray wolf, brown bear, and lynx. Migratory birds, such as the Arctic tern—which flies all the way from the South Pole each year—visit Alaska every summer to nest and feed. The waters of the state are rich habitats for polar bears, walruses, Pacific salmon, king crab, orcas, many types of seals, and beluga, humpback, and gray whales.

Yet even with Alaska's small population and vast areas of untouched wilderness, there are still threatened or endangered species in the state. Birds such as the short-tailed albatross and the Eskimo curlew are in danger of being lost forever. As a result of hunting, fishing, and pollution, marine mammals such as the Steller sea lion and five species of whales are also endangered.

Brown bears range throughout Alaska and can weigh 900 pounds (400 kg) or more.

10 KEY PLANTS AND ANIMALS

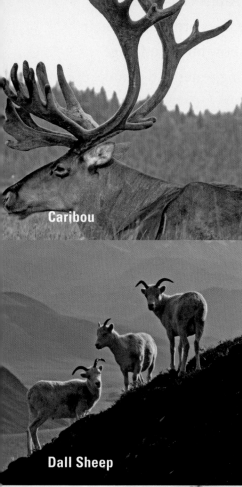

Caribou

Dall Sheep

Fireweed

1. Caribou (Reindeer)

Caribou are well adapted to living on the tundra. Their hooves work like snowshoes and help them dig for food in the snow. The hooves keep them from sinking into the mud in spring. Caribou eat willows, sedges, blueberries, and moss.

2. Dall Sheep

Dall sheep live in the mountainous regions of Alaska. They are well adapted to rugged ground and can move nimbly even on steep, rocky land. This keeps them safe from predators, who have difficulty moving over rough terrain.

3. Fireweed

This wildflower is a common summer sight in Alaska. Fireweed grows and spreads in sunny areas opened up by construction or wildfires. When trees begin to take over, the seeds lie dormant in the ground, waiting for better growing conditions.

4. Gray Wolf

Also known as the timber wolf, this species is threatened elsewhere but abundant in Alaska. Wolves live in packs and can hunt large animals such as caribou and elk. They can be black, gray, tan, or almost white.

5. Orca

The orca, also known as a killer whale, is a large, black and white marine mammal in the dolphin family. Some orca groups only eat fish, such as salmon. Others hunt in packs for seals and whales.

6. Polar Bear

Polar bears live in the waters and pack ice of the Arctic region all around the world, including Alaska. They can swim for miles, and they hunt seals, walruses, whales, and birds. Their survival is threatened by climate change and loss of sea ice.

7. Reindeer Lichen

Reindeer lichen is a gray-green plant that grows across Alaska's tundra. Lichens are fungi and algae that join together. To survive, the fungus part of the plant takes water out of the air, and the algae part makes energy from sunlight.

8. Salmon

Several species of salmon, including chinook, chum, and sockeye, live in Alaska. Most salmon spend their adult lives in salt water. They spawn, or lay their eggs, in freshwater. Brown bears feast on salmon during their spawning season.

9. Snowy Owl

Year round, snowy owls live on the open tundra. These large birds of prey nest on the ground. They hunt rodents, hares, songbirds, geese, and sometimes weasels and foxes, in the snow and over grassy meadows and marshlands.

10. Walrus

Walruses live along Alaska's coast. These marine mammals can weigh 2,000 pounds (900 kg) and have long tusks. They use them to crack breathing holes in the ice, fend off predators, and pull their own huge bodies out of the water.

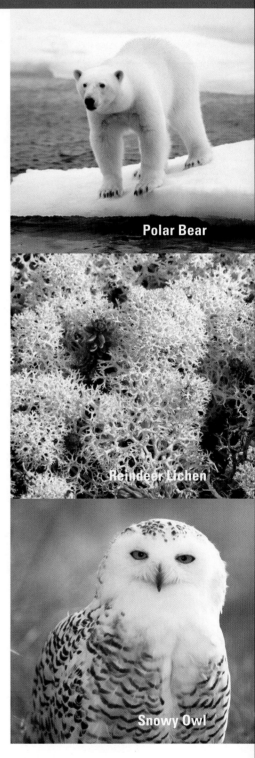

Polar Bear

Reindeer Lichen

Snowy Owl

A Native boat carver creates a Tlingit war canoe.

From the Beginning

The history of Alaska is as colorful as the wildflowers that bloom on the tundra after the ground begins to thaw in the spring. Few states can match Alaska's long, amazing saga of ancient peoples and cultures, strong traditions, hardy explorers, and daring adventurers.

Alaska's Early Peoples

During the last Ice Age, with much of North America covered by glaciers, the level of the sea was much lower than it is today. About eleven thousand to thirty thousand years ago, scientists say, the Bering Strait did not exist. This is the body of water that separates Siberia from Alaska, and it is 55 miles wide (88.5 km) at its narrowest spot. Instead, there was a "land bridge," perhaps 1,000 miles (1,600 km) wide, between the continents of Asia and North America. This area is called Beringia.

Prehistoric people from the Siberian and coastal region of northern Asia settled in Beringia. They were hunter-gatherers, and they were able to hunt very large game using flint-tipped spears. These animals moved in huge migratory herds that crossed the land bridge. The prehistoric people followed the herds of musk oxen, mammoths, mastodons, and other big game into the new territory.

The original inhabitants of Alaska followed animals such as the mastodon across a land bridge from Asia.

Most authorities think that, before the end of the last Ice Age, some of these hunters migrated by land into Alaska and beyond, perhaps traveling along the coast in an ice-free corridor. Among these hunters, it is believed, are the early ancestors of Native Americans living in Alaska today.

When the Ice Age ended, the sea rose higher and flooded the land bridge. People and animals could no longer cross on foot. But most authorities believe that new waves of people continued to arrive in the Alaska region over the next few thousand years. These people may have come across the Bering Sea by boat. Many believe that the Eskimos and Aleuts of today's Alaska are descended from these later arrivals. In any event, Eskimos and Aleuts are distinct ethnic groups, and they are not included among the Native American tribes. They are generally referred to as Alaska Natives.

The early Alaska Natives along the Panhandle coast enjoyed mild weather year-round. Lush rain forests supplied them with wood to make houses, carvings, tools, and boats. The men fished in rivers and seas filled with salmon and other fish. They also hunted seals and even whales. They often went to sea to raid rival villages. Their boats were dugout canoes, each one carved out of a single tree. The women gathered berries and roots. Ceremonies and feasts were colorful events. Craftsmen carved and painted masks. Women wove baskets and sewed fancy garments that included seeds, beads, shells, and feathers.

Other Alaska Natives lived inland on the Alaskan Peninsula. These people, known as the Athabascan culture or linguistic group, moved from place to place, usually following herds of caribou, moose, or other game. They made stone tools and weapons and, in the warmer months, lived in houses of bark that were easy to break up and transport. Besides hunting game, they caught salmon and freshwater fish and gathered berries. To prepare for the long, cold winters, they stored meat and moved into underground shelters.

Japanese Occupation

During World War II, the Japanese occupied a few Aleutian Islands. They lacked accurate information and sent a large force to take Adak Island, not knowing it was undefended. They later occupied Kiska [which had a ten-man weather monitoring group, and a few dogs] and Attu, home of forty-five Aleuts and two other Americans.

Among other Native Alaskan peoples were two Eskimo groups—the Inupiat and the Yupik. The Inupiat settled along the Arctic coastline. The men carved tools and hunting spears from ivory and bone. They fished, hunted waterfowl, and caught seals using narrow **kayaks** made from bone and hides. To capture whales and ivory-tusked walruses, they formed hunting parties. They used bigger, wider boats called umiaks. Women prepared food, made clothing, and tended their homes, made of whalebone and hides, driftwood, or snow. The Inupiat burned seal oil for fuel.

Inupiat hunters paddle their umiak in search of whales.

The Native People

The ancestors of today's Alaska Natives arrived in the area some time between 10,000 and 16,000 BCE. They came in several waves of migrations. The earliest ones spread south through North, Central, and South America. Later groups chose to remain in Alaska. The original tribes that inhabited what is now Alaska just before the time when the first non-natives explored the area include the Ahtna, Aleut, Aluutiq, Eyak, Gwich'in, Haida, Han, Holikachuk, Ingalik (or Degexit'an), Inupiaq (or Inuit), Kolchan, Koyukon, Tanaina, Tanana, Tlingit, Tsimshian, and Yupik.

Native Alaskans wear parkas made of animal skins.

These tribes were spread across huge areas, and they lived in very different environments. The environment had a large impact on their lifestyle and culture. All developed very complex ways of dealing with their particular place. The harsh climate found in much of Alaska played a role in their cultural practices. All of the tribes were primarily hunters and gatherers, but the food depended on the location. The Tlingit, who lived on the coast near lush forests, would fish for salmon, and gather foods such as berries. Tribes that lived inland might focus on hunting caribou. In many areas, vegetation was scarce. Alaskan Natives could get nutrients from organ meats of animals, such as caribou liver or seal brain. Tribes that lived in particularly cold parts of Alaska used the fur of animals to keep warm.

Russians were the first non-native people to have significant contact with the Alaska Natives. They first traded with the Aleuts, then forced them to work in the fur trade under cruel conditions. Disease killed many Alaska Natives in the first years of contact with outsiders. Later, when the United States purchased the Alaska territory from Russia, the leaders decided that the Alaska Natives did not pose a threat to American expansion. The American method used was to suppress native culture. Native languages were sometimes banned, and cultural practices were discouraged.

In recent years, many Alaska Natives have begun to revive their culture. There are 227 federally recognized tribes in Alaska. They belong to thirteen Alaska Native Regional Corporations, which manage land and financial affairs. Though some traditions have faded, members of the younger generation are trying to restore them.

Spotlight on the Aleut

The word Aleut is pronounced "al-yoot." The exact origin of the word isn't clear, though it was the Russian name for the tribe, and might have come from the Aleut word *allithuh*, or community. The Aleut (or Aleutians) call themselves *Unangan*, which means "the people."

Homes: The Aleut made homes called barabara, which consisted of an underground room with a structure of wood or bone above it. The house was covered in mats, and then in earth, to keep it warm inside.

Food: The Aleut were seagoing hunters. They hunted seals, sea lions, and whales in kayaks made from sealskin stretched over a wooden frame. They also fished using nets and harpoons. Men did most of the hunting and fishing, while women gathered plants.

Clothing: Men and women wore similar clothing. It consisted of sea otter and sea lion hides, fashioned into pants, long tunics, and **parkas**. They also wore fur mittens, and boots called mukluks that might be insulated with grass or moss. Sometimes the men would wear a parka made from puffin feathers. The waterproof feathers would help keep them dry. Kayakers wore an outer garment made from seal intestines that was almost completely waterproof.

Hair and Ornament: Men and women usually pierced their ears and noses, and they wore bead or shell jewelry. They also wore necklaces. Men and women also used paint on their faces and were often decorated with tattoos.

Art: The Aleut were renowned carvers. They made decorative and ceremonial masks from wood and carved beautiful designs in the long ivory tusks of walruses. They also wove baskets from reeds and grasses.

Living along Norton Sound, the Yupik Eskimos enjoyed a milder climate. They fished using hooks, spears, and nets, and they also hunted ducks and birds.

The earliest Aleuts settled on the Aleutian Islands. They formed a society rich in art, religion, and community life. The climate was foggy, windy, and harsh, but the land did not freeze over, and food was plentiful. The men carved beautiful tools and weapons from bone and ivory. They fished with hooks and lines and went to sea in kayaks made of bone and animal skin. Using harpoons, they hunted sea otters, seals, and sea lions. The women gathered berries and roots and walked the beaches collecting mussels, clams, sea urchins, kelp, and seaweed. Big families consisting of parents, children, and other relatives lived together in houses built underground. The women wove baskets and sewed sealskins into waterproof clothing.

Europeans Come Ashore

For centuries the rest of the world knew little or nothing about the world of these Native Alaskan peoples. That began to change after a Danish sea captain named Vitus Bering led a crew and two ships to the "land to the north" in 1741. Sailing under orders from the Russian government, Bering and his men reached the Aleutian Islands and sighted the coast of Alaska. On the trip back home, Bering and many of his crew died from scurvy, a disease common among sailors that was caused by a lack of vitamin C. A few survivors returned to Russia, bringing sea otter pelts and news that the area was bursting with valuable fur-bearing animals.

Vitus Bering, sailing for Russia in 1741, became the first European to explore the coast of Alaska.

The Alaskan fur trade became very important to Russia's economy. A Russian fur trader could earn three times a typical yearly wage with a single Alaskan sea otter pelt. By the late 1700s, Russia had become the greatest fur-trading empire in the world.

In the beginning, the Native peoples were eager to trade with the Russians for useful tools made of iron and for other goods. Some of the early contact was peaceful and cooperative. Many of the first Russian traders had Native Alaskan wives and families. But the Russians carried diseases that killed many Native people. In all, about 80 percent of all Aleutian people were killed by diseases carried by the Russians, such as tuberculosis and smallpox. Europeans and Asians had adapted to these diseases and had some immunity, but the Native Alaskans did not.

The Russian empress Catherine the Great promised good will to the Aleuts and said that Russians should treat them kindly, but this did not happen. The Russian fur companies treated the Native peoples harshly and forced them to hunt sea otters as far from home as California. Some Russian captains took Native Alaskan children hostage so that their parents would work for them. Many Alaska Natives were treated as virtual slaves. Families were forcibly divided, and any attempt at rebellion was severely punished. By the 1820s, nearly all the sea otters along the coast had been killed, and the Native population was suffering.

Near the present-day town of Sitka, the Russians established their main colony. The powerful Russian-America Company was granted rights by the Russian ruler to "all industries connected with the capture of wild animals and all fishing industries on the shore of Northwestern America." The Russians tried to keep their activities in Alaska a secret from other nations.

At this time, Russian orthodox missionaries and clergymen came to the area to spread their religion. Many Russian Orthodox texts were translated into Aleut, and even today that church has a presence in modern Alaska.

Exxon Valdez

On March 24, 1989, the oil tanker *Exxon Valdez* hit Bligh Reef in Prince William Sound, spilling up to 38 million gallons (143,845,648 liters) of oil. The spill killed as many as 250,000 seabirds, 2,800 sea otters, 22 orcas, and 247 bald eagles. More than twenty-five years later, the effects are still being felt.

Making a Totem Pole

Totem poles are important ceremonial items of the Tlingit and Haida cultures found on the Alaskan coast and the Pacific Northwest. They were usually carved from fully-grown cedar trees and could symbolize many things. Some recounted a person's life and accomplishments. Some told a legend, or the story of an act of generosity. Or they might record a spiritual or mystic experience. You can make a model totem pole to tell a story about your own life.

What You Need

A cardboard tube (such as a paper towel roll or a tubular chip can)
Construction paper
Pencil, pen, markers, and/or paint
Glue
Scissors

What To Do

- Think of a story you would like to tell. It could be a story from a book, or a family legend. Or it could be the story of you, depicting several important events from your life. Think about pictures that would symbolize the story. They shouldn't be scenes from the story, but rather characters or symbols.
- Cut the construction paper into equally sized squares so that you can fit three, four, or five figures on your pole, depending on your story.
- Draw pictures symbolizing your tale on the squares, and then glue them on, stacked in order. The totem pole can start at the top or the bottom.
- Then, tell someone your story, using the totem pole to illustrate it. Or, show someone the totem pole and see if they can figure out the story.

Between 1774 and 1793, Spain sent thirteen ships to Alaska to study the Pacific coastline. The Spanish never set up a colony, fort, or other settlement, but they mapped much of the area. They gave Spanish place names to Malaspina Glacier, the port of Valdez, and Madre de Dios Island. Explorers from Great Britain, France, and the United States also started to take notice of the region.

Early in the period, Britain had very little presence in Alaska. It had only a few scattered trading posts. British explorer Captain James Cook sailed into Alaskan waters in May 1778, hoping to find a northern shipping route between the Pacific and Atlantic oceans. Cook mapped much of the Alaskan coastline. He and his crew also carried away sea otter pelts. The crew made a hefty profit selling them in Chinese ports.

Cook's exploration of the area sparked some British interest, and their presence increased. The British-run Hudson's Bay Company set up posts at Fort Yukon, Fort Durham, and Fort Stikine.

As word about Alaska spread around the world, more ships arrived. In the early 1790s, the British explorer George Vancouver carefully mapped the Inside Passage and became the first European to spy "distant, stupendous mountains covered with snow." He was describing Denali and the Alaska Range.

Seward's Folly

In the 1800s, American fur traders began competing with the Russians. The Americans traded sugar, guns, and alcohol to the Native Alaskan peoples. Some of the Native groups used the guns to fight against Russians. The Russians proved unable to settle the region in large numbers or maintain friendly relations with the Native peoples. Tlingit Indians killed many Russian settlers.

By 1835, American whaling ships based in New England were hunting whales as far away as Alaska. While hunting in the Arctic, New England whalers met Eskimo whale hunters and learned about hunting the bowhead whale. This whale, like another species known as the right whale, was considered

Inuksuk

Inuksuks are monuments or landmarks made of stone, crafted by the Inuit, Inupiat, Yupik, and other Alaska Natives. Some are single stones standing upright; others resemble a human form. They were used to mark directions, caches of supplies, or revered sites, and stand out on an often otherwise barren landscape.

Secretary of State William Seward arranged for the United States to buy Alaska from Russia for a bargain price.

ideal for hunting because it swims quite slowly and floats after death. Native Alaskans used whale meat and blubber (a thick layer of fat) for food.

Non-native hunters used the whale's baleen, or the bristly filters the whale uses to feed on krill and other small organisms. The baleen—also known as whalebone—was used to stiffen women's corsets, and for parasol ribs. The bowhead whale was also an excellent source of oil. Before the discovery of petroleum, whale oil was an important fuel used in the United States. New England whalers were the major suppliers. In 1865, near the end of the Civil War, the Confederacy (the Southern states that had seceded from the United States) sent the warship CSS *Shenandoah* into the Pacific Ocean to hunt down New England whalers. This was done to hurt the Union's economy. In the Bering Strait alone, twenty whaling ships were sunk. Overall, the *Shenandoah* caused $1.6 million in damages in eight months.

It was clear by the 1860s that Russia was unable to protect Alaska. Russia also had growing money troubles. The nation had lost a costly war with Britain, and the fur trade was in decline. By 1865, Russian rulers were interested in selling off Alaska and US Secretary of State William Seward was eager to buy it.

Most Americans knew little about Alaska and thought of it as a faraway frozen wasteland. They called it "Seward's Ice Box" and "Andrew Johnson's Polar Bear Garden." They called the idea of buying it "Seward's Folly" (a folly is a foolish act). But in 1867, a deal was finally struck. The United States bought all of Alaska for $7.2 million, or about two cents per acre (0.4 ha). It turned out to be one of the biggest bargains in history.

Starting to Grow

Everyday life in Alaska did not change much in the first few decades after the US purchase. Few people moved to Alaska from elsewhere in the United States. Congress made no effort to set up a workable government or regulate hunting and fishing.

On October 18, 1867, the United States flag was officially raised in Alaska. At various times between 1867 and 1884, Alaska was under the jurisdiction of the US Army, the US Department of the Treasury, and the US Navy. The region was called the Department of Alaska. In 1865, the first telegraph line was installed through Alaska, meeting up with one that crossed the Pacific to Asia. In 1884, the region became known as the District of Alaska.

William Seward, the secretary of state responsible for purchasing Alaska, was one of the first tourists to visit the region. He traveled there in 1869 and reported back on Alaska's natural wonders. The naturalist John Muir toured Alaska in 1879 and wrote about the beauty of the Inside Passage and Glacier Bay, calling it a "fairyland." In the 1880s, tourists began joining the small stream of fishers, miners, and other settlers who came to the area on steamships.

In the 1890 US Census, Alaska's population was only 32,052. Of that total, 23,531 people, or 73 percent, were Native peoples. By 1900, however, the population had nearly doubled, to 63,592. The number of white settlers had jumped from around 8,500 to more than 36,500. The reason for the population increase was gold.

One of the biggest gold strikes in the region was made in 1896 along the Klondike River in Canada. By the following year, news of the strike had spread. To get to the site, herds of fortune hunters

A line of prospectors heads over the Chilkoot Pass to reach the Klondike region to search for gold.

10 KEY CITIES

University of Alaska Fairbanks

Ketchikan

1. Anchorage: population 291,826

Anchorage, in south-central Alaska, is home to more than 40 percent of the total population of the state and is a popular tourist destination. It is a major hub of air travel and shipping.

2. Fairbanks: population 31,535

The largest city in the Interior is home to the state's oldest university, the University of Alaska Fairbanks. Though large, it retains a frontier feel, and is the gateway to many smaller inland cities and villages.

3. Juneau: population 31,275

This capital city of Alaska is in the Alaska Panhandle, on the Gastineau Channel. At 2,712 square miles (7,036 sq km), it the second largest city in area in the United States. It is almost as big as Delaware and Rhode Island combined.

4. Sitka: population 8,881

Sitka, on Baranof and Chichagof Islands, has been inhabited for about ten thousand years, originally by the Tlingit. It is the largest incorporated city in the country by area, with 2,870 square miles of land (7,434 sq km), and 1,941 square miles (5,027 sq km) of water.

5. Ketchikan: population 8,050

Ketchikan began as a summer fishing camp for the Tlingit tribes and became an established town in 1885. It is the most southeasterly city in Alaska, and it is home to the world's biggest collection of totem poles.

6. Wasilla: population 7,831

Lying at the north end of the Cook Inlet, Wasilla is part of the Anchorage Metropolitan Area. The former Alaska governor and vice-presidential candidate Sarah Palin started her political career as the mayor of Wasilla.

7. Kenai: population 7,100

Located where the Kenai River flows into the Cook Inlet, Kenai uses as its motto, "Village with a Past … City with a Future." The first paved road from Anchorage didn't reach Kenai until 1956.

8. Kodiak: population 6,130

Residents of Kodiak, located on Kodiak Island, have to travel by plane or boat to reach the mainland. It is the home of the Kodiak bear, the largest subspecies of brown bear in the world.

9. Bethel: population 6,080

Located on the Kuskokwim River, Bethel is reachable only by the river, or by air. Bethel is home to the Kuskokwim 300, a noted dogsled race. The region is flat, with very few trees, and lies inside the Yukon Delta National Wildlife Refuge.

10. Palmer: population 5,937

Palmer is home to the annual Alaska State Fair and is noted for its record-breaking oversized vegetables. It is also home to the Palmer Museum of History and Art, which celebrates Palmer's history and culture and maintains two acres of public gardens.

Wasilla

Bethel

sailed the Inside Passage from Seattle, Washington, to Skagway, Alaska. Carrying a year's worth of food, clothing, and supplies, they then began a steep and dangerous trek over the St. Elias Mountains. The Skagway newspaper reported, "Miners in the Yukon require strong and rich food, and they will drink bacon grease like so much water."

The search for gold extended into other regions, where some earlier strikes had also been made, such as in Juneau in 1880. New strikes were made at Nome in 1898 and Fairbanks in 1902. Once a discovery was announced, miners, homesteaders, merchants, and real estate dealers streamed in. More than sixty thousand Americans traveled to or through Alaska during the gold rush. Many of them decided to stay.

One author helped put Alaska into the popular imagination. Jack London (1876–1914) was an American writer popular especially for his stories of the outdoors. In 1897, he joined the rush for gold in Alaska and the Canadian northwest. He didn't have any success hunting for gold. But this rugged wilderness became the setting and inspiration for some of his best-known fiction, including *The Call of the Wild*.

A statue of Baldo, one of the lead dogs in the Great Race of Mercy, stands guard in Central Park in New York City.

From Territory to State

In the early twentieth century, many of Alaska's mining and fishing camps grew into towns. Fur trading became less important, while gold and copper mining, logging, and fishing created many jobs. Roads, railroads, ships, riverboats, and telegraph lines were built to connect Alaska, in some degree, to the outside world.

But most settlements were still remote outposts, surrounded by vast wilderness. Roads were few, and mail and supplies had to be carried overland by dogsled. Margaret Murie, an Alaskan naturalist and author, described her childhood in Fairbanks: "We were all far away from the rest of the world; we had to depend on one another."

This could be seen in the famous Great Race of Mercy that delivered medicine to Nome on February 2, 1925. Children in that western city of 1,400 residents were dying of diphtheria, a serious, contagious disease. The closest life-saving vaccine was in Anchorage, more than 1,000 miles (1,600 km) away. A train took the serum to the end of the line, and dog teams and mushers covered the last 674 miles (1,085 km) in bitter cold. More than 150 dogs and twenty mushers relayed the medicine to Nome in just five and a half days, cutting in half the record for traveling the distance.

Caught in the Middle

The classic children's book *Julie of the Wolves* by Jean Craighead George is a well-known portrayal of a Yupik girl caught between traditional and modern cultures. When she flees a bad situation to live alone on the Alaskan tundra, she befriends a wolf pack to survive. The book won a Newbery Medal in 1973.

On August 24, 1912, Alaska officially became a territory.

In 1917, the United States entered World War I, and many Alaskans joined the military. After the war, in 1922, Roy Jones, a former World War I pilot, flew a small floatplane from Seattle to Ketchikan. A floatplane is an aircraft designed to land in water and float. Soon, small airplanes, many of them floatplanes, were delivering mail and other goods over long distances throughout Alaska.

Alaska's population and economy grew during the 1930s, in part because of a jump in the price of one of the territory's two biggest products at the time—gold. The other major product was canned salmon.

World War II began in 1939. The United States entered the war in 1941, after Japan attacked the US Navy base at Pearl Harbor, Hawaii. In 1942, Japanese planes bombed Dutch Harbor, on the Aleutian Islands. Japanese troops occupied two of the islands for a year before being driven out.

During World War II (1939–1945), Alaska became important as a military site, known to many as the "Guardian of the North." President Franklin D. Roosevelt ordered fuel pipelines, airfields, military bases, and roads to be built. As part of this work, US soldiers in 1942 built a highway running some 1,400 miles (2,300 km), from Dawson Creek, British Columbia, to Delta Junction, near Fairbanks, Alaska. Known as the Alaska-Canada, or Alcan, Highway, it was finished in just eight months.

Alaska continued to be important to the country's defense after the war, as tensions grew between the United States and the Soviet Union (a country that existed from 1922 to 1991 and that included Russia). Roads, pipelines, docks, railroads, and airports were built, and Alaska boomed. Families joined the workers, and soon there were many new houses, churches, and schools. The new Alaskans helped breathe life into a growing movement in favor of statehood. Despite some opposition in Congress, the necessary legislation was finally passed in 1958. On January 3, 1959, Alaska became the forty-ninth US state.

The Great Alaska Earthquake

Alaska is known for its earthquakes. Every year, it has between five thousand and six thousand—more than the rest of the United States combined. But none of them compare to the Great Alaska Earthquake.

On Good Friday, March 27, 1964 at 5:36 p.m., an earthquake struck in Prince William Sound, off the southern coast of Alaska. The earthquake had a magnitude of 9.2, which makes it the second most powerful earthquake ever recorded. The quake lasted for four minutes and thirty-eight seconds. Aftershocks in the thousands continued for months

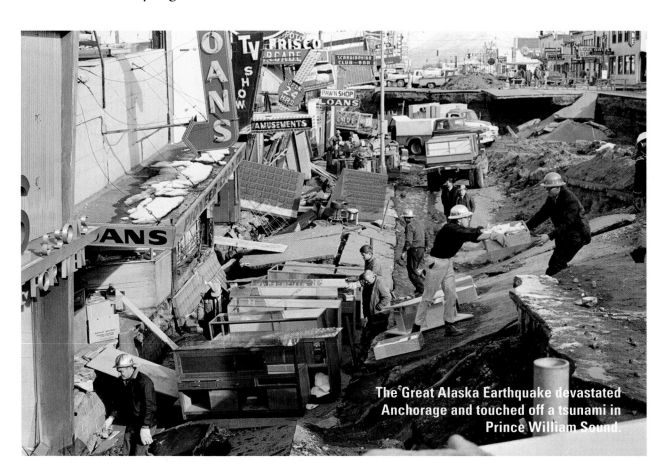

The Great Alaska Earthquake devastated Anchorage and touched off a tsunami in Prince William Sound.

after the initial quake. Some of the early aftershocks were very powerful, with magnitudes of more than 6.0.

The Great Alaska Earthquake was a type of megathrust earthquake. These occur when one tectonic plate is forced down by another plate. Tectonic plates are massive slabs of rock that move over the mantle, or rocky section, of the earth that lies above the core.

Though much of the region where the earthquake struck wasn't heavily populated, there was a lot of damage and about 139 deaths.

Buildings and infrastructure in Anchorage were heavily damaged, because most of it had not been built to withstand earthquakes. The quake triggered a massive underwater landslide in Port Valdez in Prince William Sound, killing thirty people. A tsunami, or giant wave caused by an earthquake, slammed into the village of Chenega, home to sixty-eight residents, killing twenty-three people. Other tsunamis hit areas as far away as California, Hawaii, and Japan. In Crescent City, California, twelve people were killed by a tsunami, and in Oregon, four children were killed.

The Great Alaska Earthquake was a pivotal point in earth sciences. Before that quake, the existing ideas about how the earth's plates moved and interacted were just theories. However, the earthquake provided evidence that proved the theory of plate tectonics and its role in earthquakes.

Because of its frequent earthquakes, Alaska has become a center of earthquake study. The Robert Atwood Building in Anchorage is outfitted with many sensors that monitor the building's response to seismic, or earthquake, activity.

Tsunami monitoring and early warning systems were also improved following the Great Alaska Earthquake. Though it had been known that tsunamis could travel long distances following earthquakes—and in fact, Hawaii had been warned about tsunamis after the quake—some improvements were made to warning systems for tsunamis that occur closer to the quake site. Now many areas have mapped evacuation routes, and frequent siren alarm tests to keep residents prepared. The Great Alaska Earthquake was a wake-up call to how vulnerable coastal communities can be to tsunami damage.

Energy and the Environment

Logging, fishing, mining, and **tourism** were the new state's major industries. Then, in 1968, huge deposits of oil and natural gas were discovered on Alaska's North Slope. The 800-mile (1,300 km) Trans-Alaska Pipeline, begun in 1975, was completed in 1977. It now carries oil across Alaska, from Prudhoe Bay in the north to the southern port of Valdez on Prince William Sound. There, oil tankers transport it to the lower forty-eight states.

Some seventy thousand people worked on building the pipeline. The state has grown wealthy selling oil. Oil revenues pay for most of the state budget. In addition, each Alaska resident receives an annual cash dividend from oil profits. In 2010, it amounted to about $1,300.

The Trans-Alaska Pipeline, which was completed in 1977, carries oil from the North Slope to the port of Valdez.

Opponents of the oil pipeline project were worried about its impact on the environment. Some of their fears were realized in 1989. That year, the supertanker *Exxon Valdez*, en route to California, ran aground and spilled nearly 11 million gallons (41 million liters) of crude oil into the clean, clear waters of Prince William Sound. Damage from the disaster continues to this day.

In 1980, the US Congress passed a law that protected more than 100 million acres (40 million ha) of Alaskan land as national parks, wildlife refuges, and wilderness areas. Environmentalists hailed the action. Opponents argued that too much of Alaska's land was being closed to commercial development.

Killed for Its Coat

Sea otters are mammals that live in the North Pacific waters. They are the largest members of the weasel family. Sea otters are among the few mammals to use tools. They dislodge and open shellfish using rocks. The thick fur that keeps them warm in frigid waters led to them being hunted almost to extinction.

Workers clean oil from an animal with dishwashing liquid after the massive spill caused when the supertanker *Exxon Valdez* ran aground.

In Their Own Words

"It's not like Alaska isn't wilderness—it mostly is. But most Alaskans don't live in the wild. They live on the edge of the wild in towns with schools and cable TV and stores and dentists and roller rinks sometimes. It's just like anyplace else, only with mountains and moose.
—Author and NPR radio host Tom Bodett

The 1980 law left open the question of whether to allow oil drilling in a certain area of the Arctic National Wildlife Refuge (ANWR). Those in favor of drilling argued that the oil would greatly benefit Alaska's and the country's economies and reduce the need for the United States to import oil from other countries. Many Alaskans also favored plans to build a gas pipeline from the North Slope, so that its natural gas deposits could be brought to market. Opponents argued that the economic benefits in both cases were too limited and that the projects would seriously damage the environment. More than thirty years after the 1980 law was passed, these proposals remained unimplemented and controversial.

As of 2015, there is a proposed natural gas pipeline that would move gas from the Alaska North Slope area to the Midwestern United States. Environmentalists object to this proposal, as do some Native Alaskan groups.

10 KEY DATES IN STATE HISTORY

1. Circa 14,000 BCE

The first Native peoples cross the Bering land bridge into Alaska, though most who settled in Alaska came in later waves.

2. July-December, 1741

Danish sailor and Russian naval officer Vitus Bering leads a Russian expedition exploring Alaska's coast. Czar Paul I gave the Russian-American Company, led by fur baron Alexander Baranov, a monopoly on the Alaska fur trade in 1799.

3. March 30, 1867

The United States purchases Alaska from Russia for $7.2 million in what was initially known as "Seward's Folly."

4. August 16, 1896

Gold is discovered in the Yukon, starting the Klondike Gold Rush. This brought large numbers of prospectors to Alaska and created a number of boomtowns.

5. August 24, 1912

Alaska becomes a territory and is split into four divisions.

6. January 3, 1959

Alaska becomes the forty-ninth state, with Juneau as its capital, and William A. Egan as its first governor.

7. December 18, 1971

The Alaska Native Claims Settlement Act is signed into law, granting the state's Native peoples rights to their ancestral lands.

8. March 24, 1989

The *Exxon Valdez* spills crude oil into Prince William Sound, causing an environmental catastrophe.

9. September 4, 2008

Governor Sarah Palin of Wasilla accepts her nomination as the Republican candidate for vice president. She and presidential nominee John McCain of Arizona lost the November election to Barack Obama and Joe Biden.

10. November 17, 2010

Senator Lisa Murkowski narrowly wins reelection to the US Senate as a write-in candidate.

Eskimo whalers clear a gap in the
ice so they have room to pull their
catch up on solid ice.

The People

Although Alaska is by far the biggest of the fifty states in area, it is the fourth smallest in population. Only Wyoming, Vermont, and North Dakota have fewer people. Most of the population is centered in urban, or city, areas. More than 40 percent of Alaskans live in the city of Anchorage alone. Large areas of the Alaska Interior have very few inhabitants.

Alaska has a large Native population, made up of Aleuts, Eskimos, and Native Americans. About one out of every twenty Alaskans is Hispanic. Some African Americans who first came to the state as members of the military during World War II chose to live in Alaska after the war. Today, about 3 percent of the people are African Americans, and about 5 percent are Asian Americans. In all, about two-thirds of today's Alaskan residents are white.

Many Alaskans moved to the state in search of opportunity. Only about 40 percent of people living in the state today were born in Alaska. Those who have moved to Alaska in recent years have come mostly from other states. Only about 7 percent of today's Alaskans are foreign-born.

Whether they came to Alaska from somewhere else or were born there, most current residents of Alaska seem to have adapted well and are happy to be there. Many citizens never cross the state line. Those who do say that they are going "outside." As one Anchorage woman notes, "We have a saying: 'Never come to Alaska while you are young, or you will forever spoil your eyes for the rest of the world!'"

Native Alaskans

Before 1900, Native Americans and Alaska Natives made up a majority of Alaska's population. Today almost 105,000 Native people reside in the state, making up a sizable minority. Some live and work in cities such as Anchorage and Fairbanks. There is also one Native American reservation, for Tsimshian Indians, on an island in the Alexander Archipelago, off the coast of southeastern Alaska.

But many more Native people live in small, rural villages. Often these can be reached only by boat or plane. Many village residents practice what is called a **subsistence** lifestyle. They hunt, fish, and gather or grow most of their own food. Though it is illegal for most people to hunt certain species, such as whales, some Alaska Native tribes have special permission to continue their traditional ways, so they can use the whale parts for food, equipment, and art as their ancestors did. They often barter for goods and services, much as their ancestors did. They may trap fur-bearing animals to make clothing or other goods, and create art with materials such as whalebone or walrus tusks.

The traditional lifestyle has, however, seen changes. Hunters now generally use guns rather than harpoons. Villagers often travel by snowmobile instead of by dogsled. Fishers drive aluminum boats with outboard motors instead of paddling kayaks. Even remote villages have television service, telephone service, and Internet connections.

A group of Tsimshian Indians works to raise a totem pole during a potlatch.

Village schools attempt to combine modern and traditional values. "Our kids participate in all the extracurricular activities," reports a Yupik village school principal. "They play basketball, race cross-country, and compete in the Native Youth Olympics. We even have a radio station!" At the same time, students learn the old traditions. "We teach subsistence classes in school," the principal explains. "The kids learn trap-building, net-making, boat building, all the traditional stuff you can think of!" There also are community programs that coach children in traditional dance, song, and storytelling and teach Native crafts such as blanket-weaving, basket-making, kayak-building, wood and ivory carving, and beadwork.

Permafrost and Climate Change

Permafrost is a layer of soil that remains frozen for at least two years. It covers much of the Arctic, including Alaska. Permafrost holds a great deal of the earth's carbon. If the permafrost was to melt because of global warming, it could release carbon and methane and accelerate climate change.

Northward Bound

Immigrants have always come to Alaska looking for better opportunities. The first Europeans in Alaska were Russians interested in trading furs. They built several outposts, and soon the Russian tsar (the ruler) sent missionaries to convert Alaska Natives to Christianity. The Russians built churches and set up schools for both Native and non-Native children. In Sitka and other parts of southeastern Alaska, visitors can still see Russian-style buildings and domed Russian Orthodox churches filled with gold artwork. Many town names in Alaska are of Russian origin, and there are some Alaskans today who have Russian ancestry. But Russians never

Holy Resurrection Russian Orthodox Church in Kodiak is among those left behind by the first European settlers.

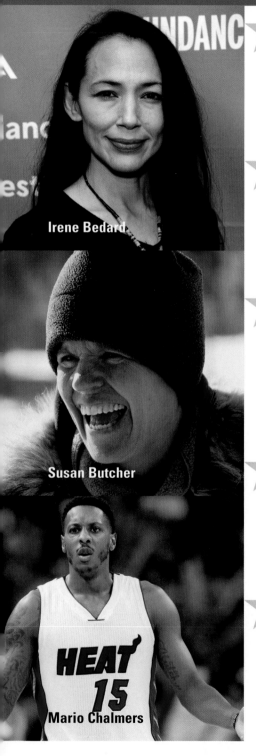

Irene Bedard

Susan Butcher

Mario Chalmers

1. Irene Bedard

This actress born in Anchorage has many Inupiat, Inuit, and Yupik ancestors. She is best known as the voice of (and model for) Pocahontas in the Disney animated movie, but she has also appeared in many other films.

2. Benny Benson

Benny Benson grew up in an orphanage. At age thirteen, he won a contest in 1927 to design the flag for the territory of Alaska. He included the Big Dipper because he'd looked at it every night before bed at the orphanage.

3. Susan Butcher

Born in 1954 in Boston, Massachusetts, Susan Butcher moved to Alaska to work with sled dogs. She won the Iditarod three years in a row and finished in the top five twelve times. She died in 2006. The Iditarod's opening day is called Susan Butcher Day.

4. Mario Chalmers

A three-time 4A State Player of the Year at Anchorage's Bartlett High, Mario Chalmers won an NCAA basketball title at the University of Kansas in 2008 and NBA titles with the Miami Heat in 2012 and 2013.

5. Carl Ben Eielson

Born in North Dakota in 1897, Ben Eielson became a pilot in Fairbanks in 1922. In 1928, Eielson and a copilot were the first to fly over the North Pole from North America to Europe. He died in 1929 trying save passengers on a stranded ship.

ALASKA

6. Ernest Gruening

Born in New York in 1887, Ernest Gruening is known as the "father of Alaskan statehood." He was the governor of the Alaska Territory (1939–1953), and an Alaska state senator (1959–1969). He fought for equality for the state's Native population.

7. Jewel

Born in Utah in 1974, musician Jewel Kilcher grew up in a remote area of Alaska. She says that the Alaskan wilderness became her greatest inspiration. Jewel sings, plays guitar, writes her own songs, yodels, and publishes poetry. She has sold close to thirty million albums.

8. Ray Mala

Born in Candle, Alaska, in 1906, Ray Mala was the first Alaska Native movie star, and he appeared in more movies than any Alaskan. Discovered at fourteen, he went to Hollywood at nineteen and worked as a cameraman and actor.

9. Elizabeth Peratrovich

Elizabeth Peratrovich was born in Alaska in 1911 to Tlingit parents. When they died, she was adopted by white Protestant missionaries. Her speech before the territorial senate in 1945 helped win equal rights for Native peoples.

10. Peter the Aleut

Born Cungagnaq, he received the name Peter when he joined the Eastern Orthodox Church. He was captured in 1815 by the Spanish and tortured to death when he did not convert to Roman Catholicism. He was named a saint in 1980.

Ernest Gruening

Jewel

Peter the Aleut

Who Alaskans Are

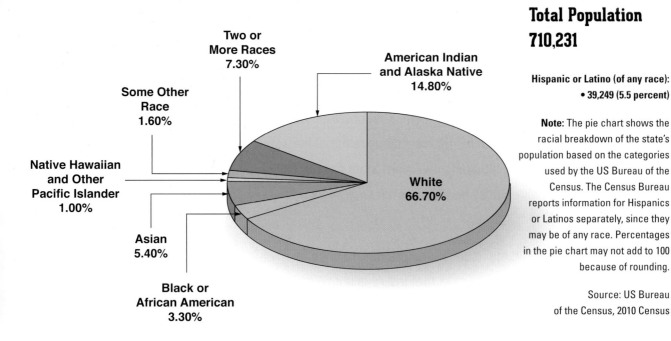

Two or More Races
7.30%

American Indian and Alaska Native
14.80%

Some Other Race
1.60%

Native Hawaiian and Other Pacific Islander
1.00%

Asian
5.40%

Black or African American
3.30%

White
66.70%

Total Population 710,231

Hispanic or Latino (of any race):
• 39,249 (5.5 percent)

Note: The pie chart shows the racial breakdown of the state's population based on the categories used by the US Bureau of the Census. The Census Bureau reports information for Hispanics or Latinos separately, since they may be of any race. Percentages in the pie chart may not add to 100 because of rounding.

Source: US Bureau of the Census, 2010 Census

settled permanently in large numbers in Alaska. Most of the early Russian settlers left when Alaska became a US possession.

The first large wave of arrivals to Alaska came in the late nineteenth century, after the Klondike gold rush. News of various gold finds had spread around the world. Fortune hunters poured in from faraway countries as well as from many parts of the United States and Canada. Each discovery of gold in Alaska brought an influx of people to remote and uncharted areas. When others followed to trade with the gold miners, the camps turned into boomtowns, or quickly built, often temporary, cities that relied on the sudden explosion of one industry. The challenges that these newcomers faced were enormous. But their ability to survive disappointment, sickness, hunger, bitter cold, storms, floods, and other hardships remains a source of pride to their descendants today.

Commercial fishing also attracted people to Alaska near the end of the nineteenth century. Fishers and cannery workers moved to the Kenai Peninsula and established the first factories in Alaska. As forts were established, American soldiers came and went. In the 1940s, the military set up permanent bases. The defense and transportation industries brought many jobs and new residents to Alaska. The population jumped from around 72,000 in 1940 to more than 225,000 by 1960.

The biggest spur to population growth was the discovery of oil, first on the Kenai Peninsula in 1957 and then in Prudhoe Bay on the North Slope in 1968. Oil field and construction jobs lured tens of thousands to the state. By 1990, Alaska's total population had reached more than 550,000. After 1990, population growth slowed, but most of the newcomers remained.

Cultural and Subsistence Harvest

Though Alaska has many regulations in place to protect native wildlife, it recognizes the need to preserve cultural traditions. It has a special system that allows some hunting outside of usual seasons for special events, such as funerals, potlatches, and ceremonies. It also allows hunting for the purpose of passing on traditions.

Alaskans, like all Americans, come from many different backgrounds and cultures. Many trace their ancestry back to Northern Europe, including Germany, Great Britain, Ireland, and the Scandinavian countries. Other Alaskans have ancestors from Italy or Poland. In recent years, increasing numbers of immigrants have come from Asia and Latin America. Today, for example, Alaska is home to Hispanics from Mexico, Asians from the Philippines and South Korea, and Pacific Islanders from Samoa.

Cities and Villages

People living in Alaska's cities have a very different lifestyle from the way of life of people in villages or the remote tundra or mountains. Yet all Alaskans learn to live with the dramatic change of seasons and the incredible wilderness around them. For example, in Fairbanks, Alaska's second-largest city in population, drivers have an unusual problem in winter—ice fog. Ice fog is a thick, white, blinding fog made of ice crystals and automobile exhaust. But Alaskans are a hardy people. They know what to expect, and cope with these conditions as best they can.

The sprawling city of Anchorage includes Chugach State Park—a 500,000-acre (200,000 ha) wilderness area. That is not to say there are no busy city sidewalks and crowds. Anchorage is a beautiful modern city in the foothills of the Chugach Mountains, with museums, shops, restaurants, and theaters. It is a center for business and finance. Anchorage is also the location of the state university's largest campus. The University of Alaska has additional campuses in Fairbanks and Juneau.

Many Anchorage residents who prefer wide-open spaces have moved an hour or more drive from downtown. But rather than hop in their cars and head out on the highway,

Many areas of Alaska must get their supplies, even pizza, delivered by airplanes.

they often fly into work. "Almost as many people who have driver's licenses have a plane," says Wasilla resident Georgia Beaudoin. "People land their float planes on Lake Hood in downtown Anchorage; it's the busiest float plane terminal in the world!" More than half of Alaska's entire population lives in or near Anchorage, but the atmosphere still feels friendly and open.

Other Alaskans live in cabins in the wilderness and rely heavily on subsistence living. They may even lack sewers or running water. Many schools located in these isolated communities are outdated and cannot afford enough teachers or new textbooks. With few roads, people often travel by boat or snowmobile. Goods must be flown in, which is expensive. Doctors and dentists are rare. People depend on health aides who can offer only basic care. Sick patients must often fly to a hospital some distance away. People living in villages count on one another to get by. "We look at family and community first," says a Yupik mother.

Festivals and the Outdoors

Alaskans by nature have a great sense of adventure and fun, and their celebrations are full of lively variety. Many of them show off the heritage of a particular ethnic group. For example, every May, Americans of Norwegian descent hold a festival in Petersburg to mark the beginning of the fishing season. The Little Norway Festival offers boat tours, traditional Norwegian costumes and dances, and the array of Scandinavian foods known as a smorgasbord.

Throughout southern Alaska, Native peoples host traditional celebrations called **potlatches**. Historically, potlatches were religious ceremonies that honored the dead. People sang, made speeches, prepared favorite foods of their ancestors, and gave away gifts. At potlatches today, people or events are honored with songs, dance, drumming, and sharing of foods such as fry bread and roasted pig. Participants also compete in fish-cleaning, net-mending, and tug-of-war contests.

Another popular event is the Native Youth Olympics, held each year in Anchorage. More than one hundred teams of Alaska Native youths compete in contests that reflect traditional fishing and hunting skills, such as the stick pull, knee jump, and seal hop.

One of the biggest festivals of the year is the state fair, held in Palmer. The Alaska State Fair is a ten-day event loaded with entertainment, contests, and exhibits. If visitors are hungry, they will find a huge variety of foods from many cultures, from Mexican tacos to fresh Bristol Bay salmon. Another long-running celebration is the winter Fur Rendezvous in Anchorage, which honors the region's early fur trappers. During this winter festival, people enjoy ice sculpture displays and a variety of contests.

Nearly all of Alaska's festivals and events celebrate the outdoors. There are bird-watching events such as the Copper River Shorebird Festival, the Sandhill Crane Festival in Fairbanks, and the Alaska Bald Eagle Festival in Haines. At the Polar Bear Jump-Off in Seward, contestants dress in silly costumes and leap into the freezing ocean. Other activities include a parade, ice bowling, and an ugly fish toss. In March, Nome holds the Bering Sea Ice Golf Tournament, during which golfers actually play a round of golf on the frozen sea.

Dog mushing—or racing on sleds pulled by teams of strong, well-trained dogs such as huskies and malamutes—is the official state sport, and throughout northern Alaska there are several major dogsled races. The most famous, of course, is the Iditarod. The 1,049-mile (1,688 km) race is run over the Iditarod Trail between Anchorage and Nome. It was organized in 1973 to honor the role of sled dogs in Alaska's history and to preserve the trail. During the Iditarod, fans come to various spots along the route to cheer on their favorite teams. Though many Alaskans spend long, cold, dark winters playing indoor sports such as basketball, they would rather be outdoors. "You can't let the weather stop you," said one visitor to the Columbia glacier. Outdoor activities are boundless—Alaskans, and hardy visitors to the state, can ski, hike, cycle, drive snowmobiles, fish, hunt, kayak, sail, rock climb, camp, and more. And in the summer, when the days are long, people get outside as much as they can.

Many people take the plunge into the harbor at Seward during the Polar Bear Jump.

10 ★ KEY EVENTS ★ ★

Alaska Bald Eagle Festival

Alaska State Fair

1. Alaska Bald Eagle Festival

In November, nature lovers flock to the Chilkat Bald Eagle Preserve in Haines to watch the world's biggest gathering of bald eagles feast on wild salmon. Other events include art displays and the release of rehabilitated eagles.

2. Alaska State Fair

Every August, thousands bring their vegetables, fruits, flowers, arts and crafts, and livestock to the fair in Palmer. There are delicious foods, games, fireworks, and concerts. Other typical attractions include a pig-herding contest, and a joke and tall-tale festival.

3. Anchorage Fur Rendezvous

This event, held in February, started in the 1900s to let trappers sell their wares. Today, it includes dozens of contests and other events, from a reindeer run and a "frostbite foot race" to a miners and trappers ball.

4. Annual Blueberry Arts Festival

This weekend of festivities celebrating Alaska's favorite fruit occurs in early August in Ketchikan. It features all things blueberry, as well as pie-eating contests, a doll and pet parade, slug races, fun runs, a beard and mustache contest, and more.

5. Gold Rush Days

This two-day celebration of mining and logging takes place in mid-June in Juneau. Visitors can watch professional miners and loggers compete, and there is also a carnival, and family-oriented activities such as gold panning, craft booths, and a food tent.

6. Iditarod Trail Sled Dog Race

On the first Saturday in March, mushers and their dogsled teams line up in Anchorage to start a race of more than 1,500 miles (1,850 km) to Nome. Fans can enjoy arts and crafts exhibitions, music, dancing, and a reindeer potluck meal.

7. Iron Dog Race

Every February, participants compete in the world's longest snowmobile race. The course stretches more than 2,000 miles (3,200 km) from Big Lake to Nome to Fairbanks. Two-rider teams battle rugged terrain and harsh weather conditions.

8. Mayor's Marathon

Racers flock to Anchorage every year on a day near the beginning of summer to run in the traditional 26.2-mile (42.2 km) "midnight sun" marathon. At this time of year, participants are able to enjoy nearly twenty hours of consistent Alaskan sunlight.

9. Sitka Whalefest

This festival, which takes place in early November in Sitka, celebrates all things related to these mighty and fascinating marine mammals. Events during the festival include whale watching trips, presentations, workshops, art, a concert, a banquet, and more.

10. World Eskimo-Indian Olympics

In mid-July, Native peoples from Alaska, the Pacific Northwest, and Canada gather in Fairbanks to compete in traditional athletic contests. Among the events are the high-kick, ear pull, blanket toss, and four-man carry.

Iditarod Trail Sled Dog Race

World Eskimo-Indian Olympics

A bronze statue of a feeding brown bear sits in front of the Alaska state capitol.

How the Government Works

4

When Alaska became an official territory of the United States in 1912, it was still ruled by Washington, DC. It did not have much control over its own affairs or any votes in Congress. The move for statehood gained momentum after World War II. A referendum in 1946 showed that most Alaskans supported statehood.

In late 1955 and early 1956, Alaskans held a constitutional congress and drafted a state constitution. The National Civic League called Alaska's constitution "one of the best, if not the best, state constitutions ever written." One feature of the constitution is that it does not attempt to achieve great detail. It leaves room for lawmakers to decide policies based on the current situation.

Alaska became a state in 1959. Like all the other states, Alaska has two US senators. But, as one of the smallest states in population, Alaska elects only one member to the US House of Representatives. These three lawmakers represent the interests of Alaska and its people in Washington.

Sitka was the first capital city of colonial Alaska, because it was where the Russian-America Company was based. But in 1880, shortly after the Americans took over, Juneau became the capital city. It has remained the capital of the state of Alaska. Ringed by mountains and surrounded by the waters of the Inside Passage, Juneau is said to be one of the world's more beautiful capital cities.

Alaskan Government

There are three levels of government in Alaska: city or town, borough, and state. Cities and towns are the smallest of these units. Alaska has about 150 cities and many more towns. Each is governed by a city council and by a city manager or elected mayor.

Alaskan boroughs, which are sometimes municipalities, are like most other states' counties. Each of the eighteen organized boroughs in Alaska is governed by an assembly and an elected mayor or a borough manager. These boroughs contain most of the state's population but take up only about 43 percent of the land area. The rest of Alaska is one huge, sparsely populated "unorganized borough," which is governed by the state.

In general, the state government is responsible for matters that affect Alaska as a whole. Transportation, the environment, business and economic growth, public health, and public safety are among the areas where the state has a major role to play. Like the federal government and other state governments, Alaska's government is made up of three branches: executive, legislative, and judicial. Each branch has its own responsibilities.

The Dimond Courthouse, at the foot of Mount Roberts in Juneau, was dedicated in 1976.

Executive

The state's governor is elected to a four-year term. He or she may not serve more than two terms in a row. The governor oversees the various departments of state government, such as those responsible for education, natural resources, transportation, and public safety. He or she appoints the officials who run many government departments on a day-to-day basis. The governor can also approve or reject proposed laws.

Legislative

The legislative branch makes the state's laws, and it budgets the money needed to operate the government. There are two parts, or chambers, to the legislature: the House of Representatives and the Senate. The house has forty representatives, elected for two-year terms. The Senate has twenty members, elected for four-year terms.

Judicial

The judicial branch has four levels of courts. The superior and district courts hold trials in both civil and criminal cases. Their decisions may be appealed to the court of appeals and the Supreme Court. The five-member Supreme Court is the state's highest court. It supervises the other courts and can declare that a law violates the state constitution. Judges are appointed by the governor, from nominees selected by the Judicial Council. The five judges vote for the chief justice, who serves a three-year term. To stay in office, judges must be approved by voters in the first election held after they have served three years. Each judge must go through a retention election every ten years.

Native Claims and Corporations

During the days of European and American settlement in Alaska, no treaties were ever signed with the Native peoples. In 1924, Congress passed a law granting United States citizenship to American Indians and Alaska Natives, without taking away tribal rights and property. But the question of how much of the land the Native peoples had rights to was left unsettled.

In the late 1950s, the US government began making use of what the Native population believed was its rightful land. The state's Native peoples formed a group to press for land rights. With the discovery of North Slope oil deposits in 1968, the issue became even more vital. In 1971, Congress passed the Alaska Native Claims Settlement Act, which gave the Native peoples ownership of a limited amount of land, 44 million acres (18 million ha), and a cash payment of close to $1 billion.

The act formed thirteen Native regional corporations and two hundred village corporations to manage the money and land. The corporations were made responsible for providing education and cultural services and for handling resources such as fishing, mining, logging, and oil drilling. Some of the corporations became very wealthy, especially those with oil on their land. All of them now play a key role in local government.

How a Bill Becomes a Law

In Alaska, citizens can propose or change a state law without going through the state legislature. The process for citizens to make a new law by themselves is called initiative. The process for them to change a law by themselves is called referendum. In either case, they must collect signatures from other people in the state. If enough people sign, the initiative or referendum measure goes before voters in the next election. If a majority votes for the measure, it becomes law.

The first occupant of the governor's official residence in Juneau was Walter Clark, the first governor of the Alaska Territory, in 1912.

Most new laws or changes in Alaska's laws come about in a different way—through the state legislature. Each proposed law, or bill, must be sponsored by a member or a committee of the legislature. But sometimes lawmakers sponsor a bill at the suggestion of a citizen or group of citizens. For example, in 1997, first-grade students at Kalifornsky Beach Elementary School, on the Kenai Peninsula, asked their state senator to sponsor a bill declaring the moose the state land mammal. He oversaw the writing of the bill, which was given a number, introduced in the senate, and eventually became law.

Sean Parnell took over as Alaska's governor after Sarah Palin resigned in 2009.

In order to become law, a bill must go through various steps. Whether it starts out in the senate or in the house, it must first be considered by committees of lawmakers in that chamber. If and when the bill is approved by the needed committees, it is voted on by the full house or senate. The members may make changes before voting. If a bill is approved by a majority of the members of one house, it moves on to the other chamber and must go through the same process.

Sometimes, the house and senate end up passing different versions of a bill. If neither chamber accepts the other chamber's version, a committee composed of members from both chambers tries to work out a compromise. The compromise bill must pass by a majority vote in both chambers before it can go to the governor.

Once a bill is passed by both houses in the same form, it goes to the governor. The governor can sign the bill, which makes it a law, or veto (reject) it. He or she may also do nothing, which means the bill may become law after a short waiting period.

A bill that the governor vetoes may still become law, but only if the two houses get together in a joint session and "override" the veto. A two-thirds, or in some cases a three-fourths, vote is needed to override a veto.

POLITICAL FIGURES
FROM ALASKA

★ Byron Mallott: Lieutenant Governor, 2014-

Businessman and politician Byron Mallott is of Tlingit heritage. He served as mayor of Yakutat and later mayor of Juneau, though he resigned after three months to serve as executive director of the Alaska Permanent Fund Corporation. In 2014, he joined forces with Independent candidate Bill Walker and was elected lieutenant governor of Alaska.

★ Sarah Palin: Governor, 2006-2009

Born in Idaho in 1964, Sarah Palin moved to Alaska as an infant. She was mayor of Wasilla, and became governor in 2006. Senator John McCain picked her as his running mate in his unsuccessful 2008 presidential campaign. Palin resigned as governor in 2009 but remained in the spotlight as a public speaker, author, and even reality-television star.

★ Frank Murkowski: Senator, 1981-2002; Governor, 2002-2006

Raised in Ketchikan, Frank Murkowski served as the state Commissioner of Economic Development before being elected to the US Senate in 1981. He was reelected three times, but resigned during his fourth term to become the state's governor. He lost his bid for reelection to Sarah Palin.

ALASKA
YOU CAN MAKE A DIFFERENCE

Contacting Lawmakers

To find out which Alaska state senators or representatives serve your community, you can visit the web site:

www.elections.alaska.gov/vi_eo_state.php

That provides a link to State Senate and State House District representatives, along with their contact information. There is also a map link so you can find out what district you live in. Registered voters can enter their information to find out more. You can call, email, or write a letter to a politician or representative to ask them a question or express your views. Writing is usually the preferred method. Remember to be polite, even if you disagree with their views. You may get a response, or you may not—but someone will read your letter, so your voice will be heard.

Protecting Women

Senator
Lisa Murkowski

When the Violence Against Women Act was passed in 2013, it was supposed to allow tribal courts to prosecute acts of domestic violence committed on tribal land against tribal women by other tribal members, or by non-tribal people. However, Senator Lisa Murkowski wanted to add an "Alaska exemption" because, she argued, Alaska doesn't have reservations like the rest of the United States. Instead, it has hundreds of villages, often without their own law enforcement. If the exemption held, a woman who had been attacked might have to travel hundreds of miles to report it. In some regions, there might be only one Alaska State Trooper every million square miles.

The tribes were outraged. If this exemption was included, many Alaska Native women would not be able to get the help and protection they needed. Concerned residents from all over Alaska brought their concerns to their elected leaders' attention. The Indian Law and Order Commission prepared a report showing how dangerous this exemption could be to Alaska Native women. Finally, Senator Murkowski changed her stance, and others followed suit. The "Alaska exemption" was repealed, and on December 18, 2014, President Obama signed the Alaska Safe Villages and Families Act into law. Now, victims of domestic violence on tribal lands are guaranteed to get help from within their own village.

Alaska fishers make the state the world's
leader in wild salmon production.

Making a Living

With its farmlands, forests, inland and offshore waters, oil fields, and mines, Alaska has a wealth of natural resources to fuel its economy and provide jobs. Alaskans also work in factories, manufacturing goods that people buy. Many Alaskans make their livings in the service sector of the economy. Some service workers are employed in schools, hospitals, stores, restaurants, or offices. Others are on the move, driving trucks or tour buses or flying planes. Some work for the state or federal government, or for their own city or borough.

Alaskan Farming

Farming seldom comes to mind when people think of Alaska, but there is close to 900,000 acres (360,000 ha) of farmland in the state. Most of it is in the Tanana Valley, around Fairbanks, and in the Matanuska Valley, northeast of Anchorage. Alaska's farmers grow hay, potatoes and other vegetables, barley, and oats, as well as greenhouse and nursery plants. Many farms keep dairy cattle, sheep, goats, or caribou. On the Seward Peninsula, Alaska Natives raise caribou for meat. Aleuts who live on the Aleutian Islands raise caribou and sheep.

Summer days provide the almost constant sunshine necessary to grow large produce in Alaska.

There was some farming in Russian Alaska. After the United States purchased Alaska in 1867, American families could settle and acquire land for farming, under the federal Homestead Act. But few farms succeeded because of the short growing season and high cost of transporting farm products to markets. When the Great Depression, a period of severe economic hardship, hit the United States in the 1930s, farmers in the Midwest and Great Plains suffered from drought, grasshoppers, and low crop prices. In a program set up under President Franklin D. Roosevelt, some two hundred farmers from Minnesota, Wisconsin, and Michigan settled in the Matanuska Valley. They got land and government aid to develop their farms and communities.

Most did not remain. But the project helped bring in others who began to think of Alaska as a place to fulfill their dreams.

Although the growing season lasts only from June through September, summer days are long. With so much sun, Matanuska Valley farmers can grow truly giant vegetables. Alaskan farmers have shown off cabbages weighing more than 70 pounds (32 kg) and at least one stalk of Swiss chard that was more than 9 feet (2.7 m) tall.

Sea Harvest

Many Alaskans work in the fishing industry. Wild salmon are plentiful in Alaska. There are five types found in Alaskan waters. One is king, or chinook, salmon. This is the largest and most valuable variety. The others are sockeye, silver (coho), chum, and pink salmon. Crab are also caught in large numbers, along with shrimp, halibut, and bottom fish such as red snapper and lingcod.

Besides the fishers who go to sea, many other people work in fishing-related occupations. There are food processors who clean, ice, and prepare the fish for market. There are also jobs in shipbuilding and ship repair, gear and tackle manufacturing and

Workers put in long days to catch king crabs in the Bering Sea.

sales, transportation of seafood, and sales of fish products. Some fishers sell their fish directly to customers on the Internet.

For several decades, the fishing industry has had ups and downs. And many jobs in the industry are only available for a part of the year. Some fishers complain about competition from fish farms that raise salmon in pens. These farms can supply markets year-round and are unaffected by weather conditions or the fish's breeding schedules. But many people who enjoy good fish say nothing tastes as great as wild Alaska seafood.

Natural Riches

There are also plenty of natural resources to be found on land. Thick, green rain forests of cedar, hemlock, and spruce cover southeastern Alaska. Loggers have harvested timber in Alaska since it was

Caribou Herding

Though some Alaskan farmers herd cows, others herd caribou. Also known as reindeer, these large animals provide meat and hides. In other parts of the world they are used for transportation. Most herds are only semi-domesticated. The herds run free most of the time, but are periodically rounded up, sometimes using helicopters.

★ 10 KEY★INDUSTRIES

Agriculture

King Crabs

1. Agriculture

About 15 million acres (6,070,284 ha) of Alaska has soil suitable for farming. Of that, about 1 million acres (404,686 ha) is currently farmed. The very long summer days help record-breaking crops grow. Livestock such as cows and caribou are raised.

2. Health Care

The health care industry includes doctors, nurses, physical and occupational therapists, administrators, health insurance workers, and more. Providence Health and Services is the biggest private health care employer in the state.

3. King Crabs

Alaska's number two seafood is the Alaskan King crab. These sweet-tasting, dark-red crabs are caught in the rough waters of the chilly Bering Sea. Crabbers often work twenty hours a day. Alaskan king crabs can weigh as much as 24 pounds (11 kg).

4. Military and Defense

Alaska is home to three Air Force bases, three Army bases, and three Coast Guard bases. The military played a big role in improving Alaska's infrastructure when it became a state, and it continues to employ many people.

5. Mining

Though most mining profits come from oil, other forms of mining make significant contributions to the Alaska economy. Alaska is well known for its gold. It also produces silver, coal, zinc, copper, sand, and gravel. Production and exploration also contribute to the industry.

6. Oil and Natural Gas

Oil and natural gas account for the largest share of the Alaskan economy. They are responsible for 34 percent of jobs in the state. The oil industry provides for the Alaska Permanent Fund, which provides a yearly check to every Alaska resident.

7. Retail

Selling goods is one of the largest industries in Alaska. Walmart/Sam's Club is the state's second biggest employer. Prices for food and consumer goods tend to be high in Alaska, because transportation is often difficult.

8. Salmon

Alaska is the top global producer of wild-caught salmon. To preserve the industry for future generations, it makes sure to use sustainable practices. Some of the employment is seasonal, so job figures vary by month.

9. Timber

Alaska has 129 million acres (52,204,448 ha) of forest. Though the timber industry in the state has declined recently, it is still a multimillion-dollar industry. Alaska produces unfinished boards, railroad ties, shingles, and other lumber products and sells them out of state.

10. Tourism

In 2013 alone, 1.96 million people visited Alaska. Most of the visitors arrived by cruise ship or by airplane, supporting the ports and transportation industry. Hotels, restaurants, resorts, and natural attractions all contribute to tourism.

Oil and Natural Gas

Tourism

Recipe for Eskimo Ice Cream

There is a traditional food from western Alaska called *akutaq*, popularly called Eskimo Ice Cream. The real version is made from whipped fat such as seal oil or caribou fat, mixed with berries. The original akutaq is high in fat but also high in healthy vitamin A and omega-3. This version substitutes vanilla ice cream for a more familiar taste and is high in calcium and vitamin C.

What You Need

One half-gallon (1.89 liters) container of vanilla ice cream or frozen yogurt
2 cups (.47 L) of blueberries or another fruit

What To Do

- Allow ice cream to thaw in the container for ten minutes at room temperature.
- When the ice cream has softened, mix two cups of ice cream with two cups of blueberries in a blender.
- Place the remaining softened vanilla ice cream in a large bowl, and stir into small chunks.
- Mix the blueberry blend loosely into the ice cream. The blueberry should be swirled through, with some parts still being pure vanilla ice cream. (The final result will be better if the ice cream isn't completely mashed and thawed.)
- Place the mix back into the original ice cream container and refreeze.

a Russian colony. After railroads and shipping ports were built during World War II, logging companies were able to deliver lumber to markets around the world. Small coastal towns prospered from this increased business.

Only a small fraction of Alaska's forestland has been harvested for lumber. In recent years, many jobs in the logging industry have been lost. At the same time, environmentalists want to protect the state's unspoiled wilderness and the wildlife that lives there. The federal government regulates logging on Alaska's public lands. It must try to balance the need for a healthy economy with the need for a healthy environment.

Minerals provide Alaska with its most valuable industry. Important minerals include zinc, gold, lead, silver, and sand and gravel. Alaska also has large natural gas deposits.

Oil is by far the greatest moneymaker, however. The oil find that changed the face of modern Alaska came in 1968, when huge oil reserves were discovered on the North Slope near Prudhoe Bay. The oil field was twice the size of any other in North America. In 1977, Alaskans finished the 800-mile (1,300 km) Trans-Alaska Pipeline over the permafrost from the Arctic Sea oil fields to the port of Valdez. About seventy thousand people in total worked on this construction project at some time, and they were well paid. Many decided to settle in the state. Today, the oil industry directly provides about forty thousand jobs in Alaska.

Once the oil began to flow, Alaska's treasury grew rich. Money from oil sales now supports about 90 percent of the state government's budget. Citizens voted to put some of the profits from oil sales into a special account called the Alaska Permanent Fund. Checks are given out each year to eligible Alaska residents for their share of earnings in the fund.

Alaska's oil production has declined by more than half since its peak in 1988. Many people want to boost production and create more jobs by drilling for oil in part of the Arctic National Wildlife Refuge (ANWR) on Alaska's North Slope. Others oppose drilling. They fear the impact of development on the unspoiled environment, especially on the life cycle of the caribou that migrate to the region each spring to bear their young. The federal government owns the ANWR, as it does most land in Alaska. The US Congress will make the final decision on drilling in the area.

Alaska Works

Most Alaskans work in some kind of service job. They provide services to others by working as doctors, nurses, teachers, bankers, restaurant workers, truck drivers, firefighters, pilots, tour guides, and more.

Many Alaskans work in defense-related industries or are members of the military. More than twenty thousand military personnel are stationed at early warning radar sites in the Arctic or on bases around the state. These bases also employ many civilians.

Tourism is one of Alaska's growing service industries. From the Gates of the Arctic National Park in the north, to the Misty Fjords National Monument in the southeast, there is much to see and do. Tourists come to watch bears feed on salmon at Katmai Falls, ride the scenic railway at Skagway, hear glaciers break up in Glacier Bay, or see the Northern Lights in Barrow. They kayak, hunt, fish, bird-watch, whale-watch, hike, and more. More than a million tourists arrive each year by cruise ship alone, and more than a half million come by air.

Although the money from tourism is welcome, there are downsides to having so many visitors. The big cruise ships are like giant floating cities, and the crowds that pour forth can overwhelm some of the places they visit. Environmentalists are also concerned

Truckers travel frozen roads to deliver goods to some areas of Alaska.

about the wastewater that ships dump overboard. To some Alaskans, tour buses and sightseeing helicopters take away from the peaceful beauty everyone came to enjoy. As visitors keep coming, communities, business leaders, and government officials are working to see that the Great Land can be enjoyed in all its splendor.

Transportation workers are key to Alaska's survival. The state is huge and far away from the rest of the world's markets. Little food is grown locally, and few consumer goods are manufactured, so these items have to be brought in from outside. Truckers battle rough, lonely, frozen roads to deliver goods to remote towns. And many places where people live and work—including the capital city of Juneau and other southeast towns such as Ketchikan, Haines, and Skagway—have no roads from outside. Travelers get there by air or by sea, often on ferries operated by the Alaska Marine Highway System.

There is only one major railroad in the state. The Alaska Railroad runs between Seward and Fairbanks. Though costly, an airplane is often the best or only way for people to get supplies and services. Many Alaskans have pilot's licenses and own planes. A bush pilot said that in the early years of flight he flew "into areas that weren't even on the map. Every flight back then was a grand adventure." Alaskans, and visitors to Alaska, will likely agree that life in America's last frontier can still be a grand adventure.

ALASKA
STATE MAP

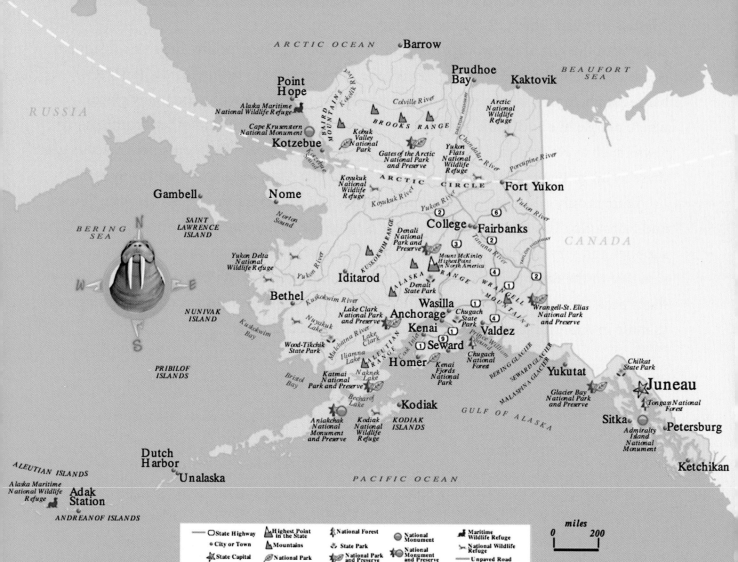

ARCTIC OCEAN • Barrow

RUSSIA

Point Hope
Alaska Maritime National Wildlife Refuge
Cape Krusenstern National Monument
Kotzebue

Prudhoe Bay
Kaktovik

BEAUFORT SEA

Colville River
BROOKS RANGE
Arctic National Wildlife Refuge

BAIRD MOUNTAINS
Kobuk Valley National Park
Gates of the Arctic National Park and Preserve
Yukon Flats National Wildlife Refuge

Gambell

BERING SEA
SAINT LAWRENCE ISLAND

Nome

Koyukuk National Wildlife Refuge
Koyukuk River

ARCTIC CIRCLE
Chandalar River
Porcupine River
Fort Yukon

Norton Sound

Yukon River

College
Denali National Park and Preserve

Fairbanks
Tanana River

CANADA

Yukon Delta National Wildlife Refuge

Yukon River

KUSKOKWIM RANGE
Iditarod

Mount McKinley Highest Point in North America
Denali State Park

ALASKA RANGE

WRANGELL MOUNTAINS

NUNIVAK ISLAND

Bethel
Kuskokwim River

Wasilla
Anchorage
Kenai

Chugach State Park

Wrangell-St. Elias National Park and Preserve

Valdez

PRIBILOF ISLANDS

Kuskokwim Bay

Nuyakuk Lake
Lake Clark National Park and Preserve
Malchatna River
Lake Clark
Iliamna Lake

Wood-Tikchik State Park

Cook Inlet

Seward
Homer

Prince William Sound

Chugach National Forest

Bering Glacier

Seward Glacier
Malaspina Glacier

Chilkat State Park

Yukutat

Glacier Bay National Park and Preserve

Juneau

Tongass National Forest

Bristol Bay
Katmai National Park and Preserve
Naknek Lake
Becharof Lake

Kenai Fjords National Park

GULF OF ALASKA

Sitka

Admiralty Island National Monument

Petersburg

Aniakchak National Monument and Preserve
Kodiak National Wildlife Refuge

Kodiak
KODIAK ISLANDS

ALEUTIAN ISLANDS

Dutch Harbor
Unalaska

PACIFIC OCEAN

Ketchikan

Alaska Maritime National Wildlife Refuge
Adak Station
ANDREANOF ISLANDS

Legend
- State Highway
- City or Town
- State Capital
- Highest Point in the State
- Mountains
- National Park
- National Forest
- State Park
- National Park and Preserve
- National Monument
- National Monument and Preserve
- Maritime Wildlife Refuge
- National Wildlife Refuge
- Unpaved Road

miles
0   200

ALASKA
MAP SKILLS

1. **What three glaciers are located near the city of Yukutat?**

2. **Which islands are home to the Kodiak National Wildlife Refuge?**

3. **Nome is on the northern edge of which body of water?**

4. **Which ocean borders the north coast of Alaska?**

5. **Which river flows from the Canadian border, across Alaska, to the Bering Sea?**

6. **Which city, known for its famous dogsled race, is near the Kuskokwim mountain range?**

7. **Which island chain that juts into the Pacific Ocean includes the Andreanof Islands?**

8. **Which line of latitude marking the beginning of the Arctic region runs through the northern third of Alaska?**

9. **What is the name of the wildlife preserve located south of Kaktovik and Prudhoe Bay?**

10. **Which city is the capital of Alaska?**

Adak Island

Arctic Circle

10. Juneau
9. Arctic National Wildlife Refuge
8. The Arctic Circle
7. The Aleutian Islands
6. Iditarod
5. The Yukon River
4. The Arctic Ocean
3. Norton Sound
2. Kodiak Islands
1. Bering Glacier, Seward Glacier, and Malaspina Glacier

State Flag, Seal, and Song

An Aleut seventh grader named Benny Benson submitted the winning entry in a contest to design the Alaska flag. The Alaska Territory first adopted Benny's design in 1927. It has a blue background, the color of the Alaskan sky and the color of Alaska's official flower, the forget-me-not. Scattered against the blue are seven gold stars, representing the Big Dipper, the brightest stars in the constellation Ursa Major ("Great Bear"). The stars represent Alaska's strength. They lead to an eighth star, the North Star, representing the northernmost state.

The state seal was designed in 1910, when Alaska was still a territory. Inside a silver circle, it shows the northern lights glowing over tall mountains. The inside of the circle also has several images suggesting different sources of the state's great wealth, including a smelter to represent mining, a train and ships, timber, and a farmer with a horse and some wheat. The rim of the circle shows a seal and a fish, representing wealth from the sea.

Alaska's state song, "Alaska's Flag," was composed by Eleanor Dusenbury with lyrics by Marie Drake. Adopted on February 23, 1955, it explains the symbolism of the state flag. The song also makes references to the blue water around Alaska, and the gold of rising sourdough, a popular bread in Alaska. To see the lyrics and listen to the song, visit:

www.alaska.net/~surlyc/ACWD/alaskaflagsonglyricsandhistory.html

Glossary

caribou	A species of deer that lives on the tundra and in subarctic areas; also called a reindeer.
delta	The usually fertile, sediment-filled area where a river empties into an ocean or other body of water.
fjord	A deep channel of a sea located between tall cliffs.
glacier	A mass of ice that forms and flows very slowly.
gold rush	A swift relocation of large numbers of people to an area where gold has been found.
kayak	A light-framed, watertight canoe originally used by the Inuit, but now adapted for use elsewhere.
parka	A warm coat or jacket with a hood; in some Alaska Native cultures, parkas are made from animal pelts.
permafrost	A layer of subsoil that remains permanently frozen throughout the year.
potlatch	A ceremonial feast that displays wealth or prosperity; presents might be given, or valuable objects destroyed to show wealth or increase prestige.
rain forest	A dense and diverse woodland characterized by bountiful rainfall; often tropical, but sometimes found in temperate zones.
subsistence	Supporting one's self by hunting or living off the land.
totem pole	A wooden pillar carved with symbols that tell a story or honor ancestors, great deeds, or gods.
tourism	Organized travel or visits to places of cultural, natural, or other interest.
tundra	Flat, treeless Arctic plains in which the ground under the top later is permanently frozen.

More About Alaska

BOOKS

Devine, Bob. *Alaska: A Visual Tour of America's Great Land*. Washington, DC: National Geographic, 2014.

Doak, Robin S. *Subarctic Peoples (First Natives of North America)*. Chicago: Heinemann Library, 2011.

Edwardson, Debbie Dahl. *My Name is Not Easy*. Seattle, WA: Skyscape, 2011.

Gill, Shelley. *Alaska's Dog Heroes: True Stories of Remarkable Canines*. Seattle, WA: Sasquatch Books, 2014.

WEBSITES

Alaska Native Heritage Center:

alaskanative.net

Official State of Alaska Government Website for Kids:

www.alaska.gov/kids

US National Park Service: Alaska:

www.nps.gov/akso/index.cfm

ABOUT THE AUTHORS

Ruth Bjorklund, a regular author for Cavendish Square Publishing, lives on Bainbridge Island with her husband and two children. She is two ferry rides from Skagway.

William McGeveran, a freelance author and editor, is the former editorial director for World Almanac Books.

Laura L. Sullivan, author of books for children such as *Under the Green Hill* and *Love by the Morning Star*, has co-written the upcoming romantic mystery *Girl About Town*.

Index

Page numbers in **boldface** are illustrations. Entries in **boldface** are glossary terms.

Index